How to Talk to Dads

BY ALEC GREVEN

ILLUSTRATIONS BY KEI ACEDERA

Collins
An Imprint of HarperCollinsPublishers

A generous donation has been made by Alec Greven and HarperCollins to support Stand Up To Cancer, a program of the Entertainment Industry Foundation to raise awareness and funds to accelerate groundbreaking cancer research.

Collins is an imprint of HarperCollins Publishers.

How to Talk to Dads
Text copyright © 2009 by Alec Greven
Illustrations copyright © 2009 by Kei Acedera

Library of Congress Cataloging-in-Publication Data
is available.
ISBN 978-0-06-172930-0 (trade bdg.)

Typography by Ray Shappell
09 10 11 12 13 LP/WOR 10 9 8 7 6 5 4 3 2 1
❖ First Edition

CONTENTS

INTRODUCTION

This book has everything you need to know about the big guy in your life—Dad.

There are all kinds of dads. Maybe yours lets you get away with everything. Maybe he's tough—tougher than Mom! Maybe he talks a lot about goals for your future.

Don't worry. You will find out everything you need to know about Dad right in this book. If you're lucky, it might help you stay out of some sticky situations, if you know what I mean.

So what are you waiting for? Turn the page!

CHAPTER ONE

Dad's Way

{ *Dads are softies with little girls because they are all cute and sweet.* }

Dad's way is a little different from Mom's. Some kids think Dad's way makes it easier to have fun, like getting to play Wii a lot more.

But if you think Dad is an easygoing guy who's going to let you run wild, then you are wrong!

Dads expect you to work hard, because life isn't easy.

Dads are easier on little kids and harder on older kids.
Everyone knows that Dads are softies with little girls because
they are all cute and sweet. You just have to live with that
if you are a boy.

TIP: *Dads let girls get away with a lot more stuff, except anything to do with dating or boys.*

Dad also sweeps things under the rug more than Mom. Sometimes he won't tell Mom if you did something wrong, like having bad behavior at the doctor's office, especially if you shaped it up.

Dad thinks about things longer than Mom, but in the end he usually follows Mom's opinion. If Mom is happy, then so is Dad.

CHAPTER TWO

The Two Sides of Dad

{ Try to keep Dad on his good side. . . . You could get rewards. }

Dad has a good side and a bad side. It totally depends on his mood and your attitude.

If you have above and beyond behavior, Dad will go to the good side and you could get rewards. If you are on bad behavior, Dad will go to the bad side. Then all you get is trouble.

Try to keep Dad on his good side. If he goes bad, get him back immediately. Dads are no fun when they are in the dark side.

In some ways Dads are tough. They don't let you quit, and they make you do things by yourself.

In some ways Dads are easy. If you want to do something, ask Dad first instead of Mom, like if you want to play a T-rated video game or drink soda instead of milk at dinner.

TIP: *There is an 80 percent chance that Dad will say yes when your mom might say no!*

Unfortunately, Dad likes to leave a lot of the decisions up to Mom.

CHAPTER THREE

What Dads Like

{ *Dad expects you to do things even when he doesn't ask. . . .* }

Dads like honest, helpful, good kids.
Dad expects you to do things even when he doesn't ask,
like cleaning your room and doing your chores.

Dads like nice manners.
They are also very picky about looking people in the eye and
shaking hands when you meet them.

Some dads love camping, especially in your backyard.
It means a lot less work for Dad, because he doesn't have to drive
anywhere and if you have bad behavior he can just send you inside.

Video games calm Dad down and put him in a better mood. This is a good way to get Dad back to his good side.

TIP: *If you and your dad get into a fight, 75 percent of the time you will make up when you play video games together.*

CHAPTER FOUR

What Dads Don't Like

{ *Dads don't like whining.* }

Dads don't like wild kids and bad behavior.
If you do something really bad, like push your sister off of the slide,
Dad will be very mad at you and there could be some yelling.

Dads don't like it when you protest.
If your dad asks you to do something, just do it.
He'll make you do twice as much if you complain.

Dads don't like whining—it puts them in a very bad mood.

Dads really don't like the "Mom lets us" trick.
Say Dad gives you one scoop of ice cream and you tell him Mom
lets you have two. Beware! If it is not true, you are asking for trouble.

Also, many kids try asking Dad after Mom tells them no.
This never works out well.

TIP: *Moms and dads usually know when you are dishonest. If you get*
caught, you will have mad parents, room time, and loss of toys.

CHAPTER FIVE

How Dads Bug Their Kids

{ *Score 1 for Dad.* }

One thing that bugs kids is when Dad doesn't let you quit, even if you are having trouble with something.

But Dad is smart—he'll look really depressed and then
you will want to restart the thing that you wanted to quit
just to make him happy.
Score 1 for Dad.

Or sometimes your dad wants you to do something
and you want to do something else.
Maybe Dad tells you that you can choose to do your homework first
or play at your friend's house, then do your homework.
Dad tells you to do whatever you want. But he doesn't really mean it.
You know what decision you are supposed to make.
Score 2 for Dad.

Another trick Dad uses is the fake conversation. Dads usually know when you are eavesdropping, and they use this against you.
They will make believe a call to the school and say something like "He's not helping his mother with the laundry. He's going to have to come to school in his underwear."

You become the best laundry helper in the family.
Score 3 for Dad.

TIP: *80 percent of dads do this trick. 60 percent of kids fall for it.*

CHAPTER SIX

How Kids Bug Their Dads

{ *When it comes to tattling, proceed with caution.* }

One thing that really bugs Dad is tattling.

When it comes to tattling, proceed with caution.
Don't risk it unless it is serious. If you see your brother and
sister using glitter glue to stick art to the floor, you should
let your dad know. That can be a clean-up nightmare.

But if your brother and sister are wrestling over a toy,
stay out of it.

Also, don't ever tell on Dad to Mom, like if you see Dad drinking out of the milk jug and not using a glass. And if Dad lets you play an inappropriate video game, do *not* tell Mom!

TIP: *If you tattletale, there is a 75 percent chance you will get in trouble too.*

Kids also bug their dads by not listening. This is big, take it from me! Even if you aren't interested, you have to pay attention.

Say Dad wants to teach you the history of the lightbulb. Look him in the eye and nod your head while he is talking. You can think about something else, but you have to say things like "Really?" or "Wow, I didn't know that!"

Don't nag your dad if he can't play with you. When you want to play, go up to him and ask nicely. But keep in mind that for any answer (yes, no, or maybe) you should say the same thing: "Okay, Dad."

Never bug or complain. This sends Dad to the dark side immediately.

Dad's Dark Side

CHAPTER SEVEN

The Power of the Father

{ *Your dad helps you become you.* }

Dad wants you to do things on your own and be a good kid.

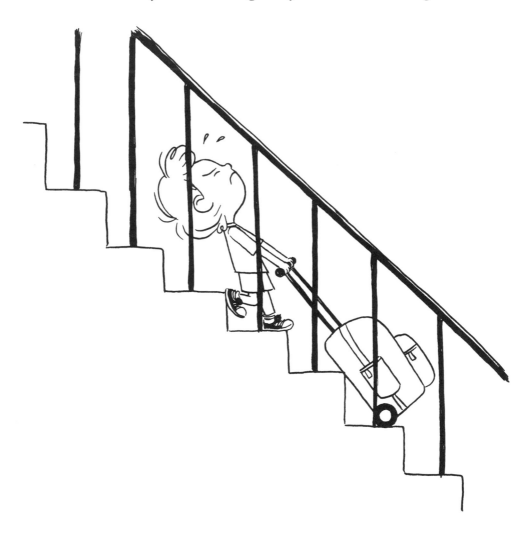

When you want to quit, Dad won't let you. When you fall off your bike, he will help you up but then make you get right back on. You have to keep going and learn that you can do it.

If you are playing chess, Dad won't go easy on you. He will play for real but help you with tips and tricks. He makes it tough so you learn and become confident.

Dad helps you make the right decisions. Unless it is something that could hurt you, he will probably let you try it and see how you do.

Dad also likes you to learn from your mistakes. He might let you keep throwing your toys up in the air as high as you can and not say anything. Then a toy hits you on the head. Dad will say, "Bummer."

Dad's goal is for you to grow up and be proud, confident, happy, and safe. He teaches you to believe in yourself and never give up. It's his job as a dad, but I think he likes doing it a lot!

Do not underestimate the power of the father.
Your dad helps you become you.

DEDICATION

For my dad, of course!